MAKING THINGS

MELANIE RICE

ILLUSTRATED BY
CHRIS BARKER

ADVISER
BETTY ROOT

Kingfisher Books

Kingfisher Books, Grisewood & Dempsey Ltd,
Elsley House, 24–30 Great Titchfield Street, London W1P 7AD.

This edition published in 1990.
Originally published in hardcover in 1985 by Kingfisher Books as
part of a one-volume book entitled *Play Together Learn Together*.

Reprinted 1990

BRITISH LIBRARY CATALOGUING IN PUBLICATION DATA
Rice, Melanie
Making things.
1. Activities for pre-school children — Manuals — For parents
1. Title II. Series
790.1'922

ISBN 0 86272 500 3

Printed in Spain.

Editor: Jacqui Bailey
Assistant Editor: Deri Robins
Design: The Pinpoint Design Company
Photography: Rex Caves
Cover Design: Nigel Osborne
Cover Photography: Mark French

Acknowledgements:
The author would like to thank her husband, Chris, for all his
invaluable advice and support during the preparation of this book.
The publishers would like to thank the staff and pupils of Hadrian
Lower School, Dunstable, for their help with some of the projects in
this book.

Contents

To parents

The 'Play Together, Learn Together' series is a compilation of ideas drawn from my experience of bringing up two young children. It was then that I discovered first hand just how long the hours can seem between breakfast and bedtime! With household chores and demanding minds competing for my attention all day, I usually found that despite good intentions, a backward glance showed how very little of my time was spent actually playing with the children. I hope that these books will provide parents who also have 'good intentions' with a source of reference; inspiring them to make the most of the rewarding hours spent in the company of their pre-school children.

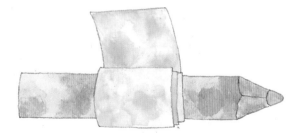

Parent and Child Together

As the series title suggests, play should always be to the mutual benefit of child and parent. Parents learn a great deal about their children by observing them while they play and by listening to them recalling their experiences. Listening is particularly important; while it is easy to talk to children, listening requires more patience — it's all too tempting to interrupt or finish sentences which seem to falter or stray from the point.

Children learn from their parents through conversation as well as through other stimuli — poems, pictures, games and so on. And because of the special intimacy which exists between parent and child each activity can be directly related to the world they share.

But do remember that the emphasis in these books is on the word 'play'. Children learn much more quickly and easily when they are absorbed and interested in what they are doing. Never force your children into an activity; if they begin to get bored, do something else. Children are also quick to pick up on the moods of their parents, so if you are bored that is another good reason to do something else.

Using This Book

In making the selection of activities for this book I have tried to include only those which are readily accessible, which generally need little preparation and use materials close to hand, and which do not require special outings to provide stimulation.

The activities have not been arranged according to age; this type of categorization seemed irrelevant to me, as every child has a different rate of development. No doubt you too will have been irritated by being told that a 'three-year-old should be able to ...' when it's clear that, whatever the activity, children proceed at their own pace. While no amount of pushing can force them to begin learning before they're ready, once they've started it is impossible to stop them.

What Will They Learn?

The ideas in this book have been designed to help children acquire a wide variety of skills, enabling them to explore and interpret the world for themselves.

Manual dexterity. The practised use of tools, such as paintbrushes, pencils and scissors, develops coordination and helps prepare children for the difficult skill of writing.

Problem solving. By handling materials, such as clay, paint, paper and card for themselves, children begin to learn about their properties and the different uses they can be put to.

Speaking and listening. Vocabulary increases with the desire to express newly-acquired knowledge. Children should be encouraged to talk about what they have made.

Observing. Close observation of colour and pattern, learning to distinguish between different shapes and understanding their relationships on the page — these early skills are very important when children come to read.

Imagination. Creativity is stimulated by giving children the freedom to explore colours, shapes and textures.

A Few Tips

Before starting a play session, bear the following in mind:

1. Atmosphere — a happy relaxed atmosphere is essential if a child is going to benefit from the session.
2. Timing — a tired or hungry child will be inattentive, while interruptions spoil concentration.
3. Location — some activities need plenty of room, others are messy and mopping up equipment needs to be on hand.

During a session:

1. Encouragement — constant praise, even for the smallest achievement will help develop a child's confidence and ability to learn new things.
2. Striking a balance — it's not easy to sit back and watch children explore and discover without succumbing to the temptation of imposing one's own ideas in order to speed up the process. Yet only by probing for themselves can children come to a real understanding of the world. Try to work alongside the child rather than lead.
3. Pace — introduce new ideas slowly and carefully and give plenty of practice with any new skills.
4. Success — don't dwell on things which seem difficult. Instead, find something your child is comfortable with and can be positive about.

And afterwards:

Sharing — display the best work for friends and other members of the family to see and admire.

Finally, remember that for both of you the main thing is that the whole exercise should be tremendous fun.

Gathering materials

Here are some ideas for building up your 'art box', but no doubt you will have plenty of others of your own.

As a general rule, introduce things to your child gradually—too much to choose from at any one time can be overwhelming. Occasionally put things away for a few months to prevent boredom.

To begin with, look around the house—even rubbish may turn out to be useful—so start collecting:

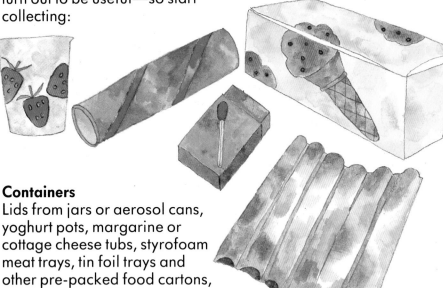

Containers
Lids from jars or aerosol cans, yoghurt pots, margarine or cottage cheese tubs, styrofoam meat trays, tin foil trays and other pre-packed food cartons, eggboxes, matchboxes, cupcake cases, tins—such as cocoa or plaster tins, with firm lids—and plastic bottles.

Paper
Newspaper, magazines, catalogues, old Christmas and birthday cards, postcards, tissue paper, foil, paper doilies, gift paper, computer print-out paper, wallpaper, cellophane, and straws.

Cardboard
Backs of notepads, corrugated card, toilet-roll cores, shirt card, cereal boxes.

Material Scraps
Any kind, but especially fur, tweed, lace, hessian, velvet, corduroy, old shirts or sheets, rug scraps, feathers, fringing, ribbons, sponge, wool.

Odds and Ends
String, shoelaces, rubber bands, pipe cleaners, buttons, beads, curtain rings, sequins, seeds, nuts, cereal, macaroni, cotton reels, iced-lolly sticks, toothpicks, woodshavings, corks, metal foil and plastic bottle tops.

Paint
1 Large plastic bottles of poster paint. Only put out a little to use at a time.

2 Powder paint. This is cheaper but messier. Mix it yourself to the thickness of double cream. If it dries out, add a few drops of hot water and leave for a couple of hours.

3 Water colour blocks. These come in boxes and are economical and clean to use. But they aren't good for experimentation with textures and are ineffective on top of coloured paper.

Painting Tips
When mixing paint it tends to go further if you add a few drops of cellulose wallpaper paste to it.

If you add a little detergent to paint it makes it easier to remove from clothes.

If you run out of paint, use flour mixed with water and food colouring.

Palettes for Holding Paint

Use yoghurt pots (or the tops of aerosol cans) placed on a tray. Or use an old baking tray with separate compartments.

> **Warning:** *When children first paint they splash their brush enthusiastically from one pot to the other until the paints become muddy. Don't interfere—they will soon realize that it's better to keep the colours separate.*

Paste

1. Wallpaper paste. Cheap and useful for sticking paper together and for thickening paint.
2. Flour and water. Mix to a stodgy consistency.
3. PVA adhesive. Buy ready-mixed or in powder form. It sticks just about everything and washes out with water.

Brushes

1. Buy large sizes to encourage bold brush strokes.
2. Sometimes use 1 inch (about 2.5 cm) hardware brushes—they can be better than art brushes.
3. Keep a separate brush for paste, or use a piece of card.

Wash all brushes in soapy water when finished with, and store them flat in newspaper to keep their shape.

Crayons and Chalks

Buy extra-thick wax crayons and the thickest types of chalk and charcoal (they don't break so easily). Peel off any paper so that the sides can be used as well.

Clay or Dough

1. Clay of a type which hardens without being baked is now available, but it is very expensive.
2. Plasticine or 'Play Doh' is softer and easier to manipulate. You can make your own. At first, use the recipe that is given here, but later try experimenting with the amounts. It will keep indefinitely in an airtight plastic bag or pot.

Dough Recipe
2 cups flour
2 tbs cooking oil
1 cup water
1 cup salt
Add paint or food colouring as wanted.

Be Prepared

Before you start any kind of art activity, spread a large sheet of polythene across the floor. It can be bought quite cheaply by the metre from hardware shops and is well worth the money. Have a large bowl of soapy water, a sponge and a mop handy!

Painting

Think of different ways to apply the paint. Spatter and splash it on. Use your fingers (most children do naturally when they begin painting), or any of the following: a comb, a brush, a piece of card, a sponge, a toothbrush, string. Try putting some paint into the corner of a plastic bag. Cut a small hole in the bag and let the paint dribble onto the paper.

Experiment with interesting textures. Add soap powder, washing-up liquid, flour, sugar, sand, PVA adhesive or wall-paper paste to the paint and see what happens.

Vary the surface you paint on. Try foil, corrugated card, tissue paper, old magazines or newspaper, wet paper, paper brushed with cooking oil, or even cellophane—the finished product can then be hung on the window.

How to Teach Painting

The answer is, don't. It impedes natural creativity. The best you can do is to provide the materials and opportunities to stimulate the imagination and then take a back seat. Avoid asking questions like 'What is it?', or 'Tell me about it', when you are presented with a piece of paper apparently filled with meaningless splodges. When children paint they are expressing their feelings rather than representing particular objects; it is the act of painting that is important, rather than the finished product.

Blobbing Paint

Drop a few blobs of very thin paint onto a piece of paper and tilt it to form rivulets. As an alternative, blow paint over the paper with a straw.

Bubbles

While you have a pot of thin paint to hand, mix some washing-up liquid into it and blow air into the pot through a small straw to make coloured bubbles on the surface. When you have a fairly frothy surface, gently lay a piece of paper over the top.

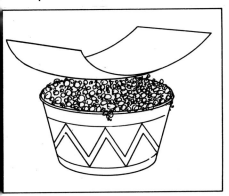

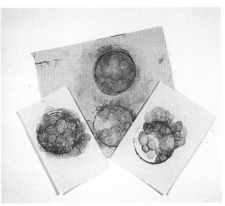

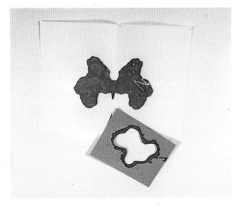

Stencils

A piece of sponge is ideal for applying paint to stencils.

1 Cut a random shape from the middle of a thick piece of card. Lay the card on a piece of paper and use it as a stencil by filling the hole with paint. Or, put the shape on the paper and paint around its edge.

Try folding the paper in half and smoothing your hand firmly over the top. On opening the paper, both sides will be identical.

2 For more intricate stencils use paper doilies. You can make your own by folding a circle of paper into quarters (as shown below) and cutting out a few simple shapes.

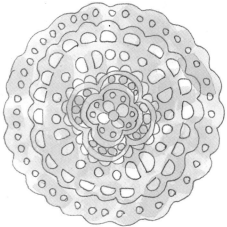

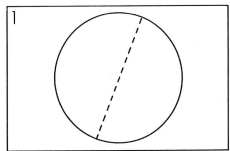

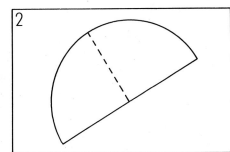

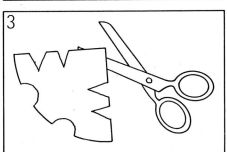

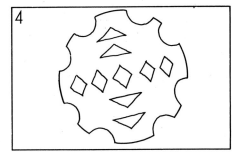

Magic painting

1 Place a thin piece of paper over any objects which have an interesting surface texture. Then rub firmly across the paper with the sides of a crayon until the pattern of the object appears.

2 With a spot of glue to stop them from slipping, stick some large magazine pictures onto a piece of card and cover with a sheet of white tissue paper. Paint water over the tissue, using a large brush, and watch the pictures appear.

3 Make a drawing with wax crayon, pressing heavily on the crayon. Wash over the paper with thin paint—the drawing will shine through.

For extra magic, follow the same procedure but this time use a white candle to make the drawing. The drawing will not show until the paint is applied.

4 Cover a sheet of strong paper or white card with brightly-coloured patches of wax crayon. Now completely cover the whole paper with black crayon. Scratch away the black to form patterns. You will need to use something with a fairly sharp point, such as a knitting needle.

Finger painting

Mix flour and powder paint with water to make a thick paint. Spread onto a sheet of firm paper, a smooth tray, or a baking tin, and let your child draw patterns in the paint with their fingers.

Colour Mixing

For older children. Put out two or three colours. Let your child decide which colours to use where. Talk about the different colour combinations he or she has made.

Making prints

First, you will need to make a paint pad. Mix some thick paint and add a pinch of wallpaper paste and a little detergent. Lay a piece of sponge or foam, or a piece of flannel in a tray (use a styrofoam meat tray or an old baking tray) and pour the paint over the sponge.

All kinds of objects will make prints. Press them firmly onto the paint pad and then onto the paper.

String Prints

1. Dip a piece of wool or string into the paint. Lay it on the paper with one end hanging over the edge. Fold the paper in half and, with one hand laid gently on top, slide out the piece of string.

2. Cover a cardboard tube with glue and wind a piece of string around the outside of the tube. When the glue is dry, roll the tube across the paint pad and then across a sheet of paper.

3. Dab PVA adhesive onto a piece of paper. Drop a few odd lengths of string onto the glued paper so that they fall into curled patterns. When the glue is dry, apply thick paint to the string. Take a print of the string pattern by placing another sheet of paper on top of the string and pressing down firmly with a rolling pin.

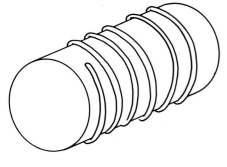

Hand and Foot Prints

Press feet and hands first onto the paint pad and then onto a large sheet of paper. Use fingerprints too, to make up a pattern.

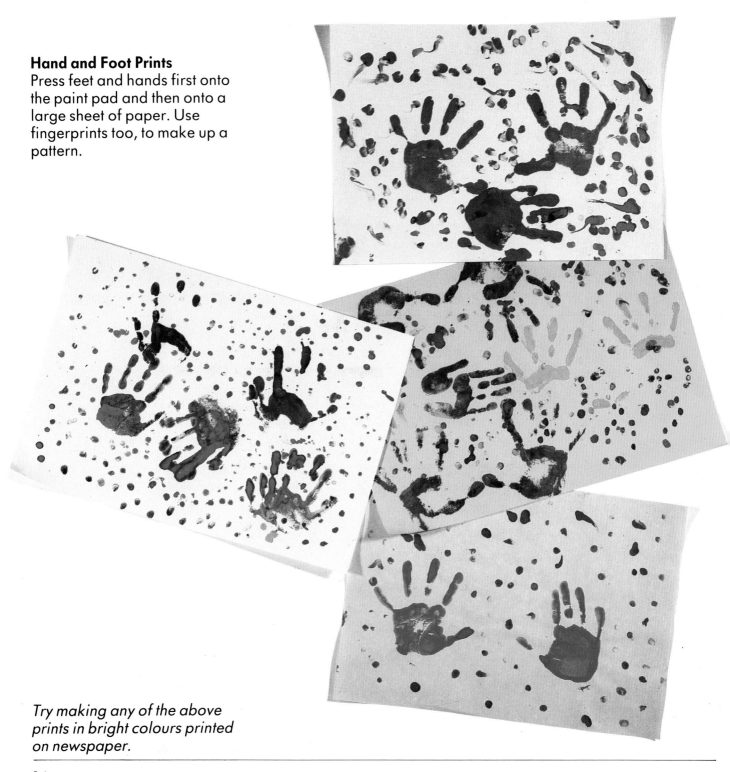

Try making any of the above prints in bright colours printed on newspaper.

Printing from Plastic

Spread a thick layer of paint mixed with PVA adhesive onto a piece of polythene. Scrape away patterns in the paint with a piece of card. Take a print by placing a sheet of paper over the polythene.

You can clean the polythene with washing-up liquid, but as you do so, take a print of the bubbles and swirls that form when you add the detergent.

Oil on Water Prints

Half-fill a baking tray with water. Add some oil paints of different colours, or left-over household paint (but keep a solvent handy). Stir the water gently with a stick, and float a sheet of paper on the surface for half a minute. Then lift the paper at one corner and peel it off the water. Lay the paper flat to dry.

Warning: Household paint can often contain lead solvents and should never be used without supervision.

Collage

For young children, simply spread PVA adhesive over a piece of paper and place objects onto the surface.

Use buttons, wool, fabrics, pipe cleaners, feathers, bottle tops, seeds, dried peas, leaves, egg shells, etc.

Use different materials as a base: card, wood, or even a slab of dough, for example.

Older children can apply glue directly to the objects. Paint some objects before gluing them, or alternatively, paint over and round them onto the paper when the glue has dried.

String Collage

String, dipped into a thick mixture of paint and paste, will stick firmly as it dries.

Paper collage

A wide variety of shapes and textures can be obtained just from paper. Remember that it can be torn, cut, rolled, twisted, bent, folded, crumpled, fringed, pleated and curled.

Pleating
Lightly mark off a piece of paper into equal divisions. Fold along the marks.

Fringing
Alternatively, cut the paper three-quarters of the way along each division.

Spirals
Cut paper into a rough circle and mark out as shown. Cut along the marks and hang it vertically from the centre. Or, fasten at both ends so that it winds horizontally across the collage like a snake.

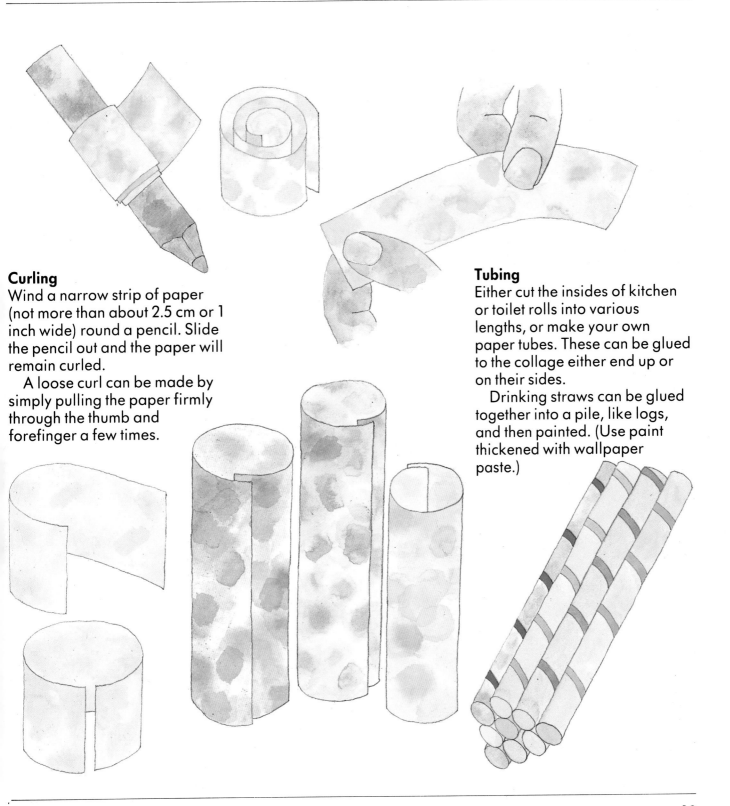

Curling

Wind a narrow strip of paper (not more than about 2.5 cm or 1 inch wide) round a pencil. Slide the pencil out and the paper will remain curled.

A loose curl can be made by simply pulling the paper firmly through the thumb and forefinger a few times.

Tubing

Either cut the insides of kitchen or toilet rolls into various lengths, or make your own paper tubes. These can be glued to the collage either end up or on their sides.

Drinking straws can be glued together into a pile, like logs, and then painted. (Use paint thickened with wallpaper paste.)

Paper patterns

Collect an assortment of paper, such as tissue paper, typing paper, silver foil, scrap paper, sugar paper, cardboard, cellophane and printed paper (newspapers, magazines, old letters, wrapping paper).

1 Make patterns using paper cut into one particular shape, such as all stars, or all circles.

2 Buy some clear plastic film which has a sticky 'peel-off' backing (you can get this from most art shops or good stationers). Tear up some pieces of tissue paper and apply them to the sticky side of the plastic. New colours can be made by overlapping two pieces of differently-coloured tissue. The final result can then be hung against a window so the light will shine through.

3 Cut silhouette shapes from black paper and stick them onto a coloured background. Or, you could colour in the background first with a finger painting.

Models

A young child can produce exciting sculptures and models using items from your art box; it does not matter at all if the early attempts are not recognizable.

Try making trains, cars, boats, people, monsters, etc. Allow your child's imagination to run riot—and before long, better models will appear than I could ever suggest.

Use cardboard boxes (for bases), tubes (for bodies or funnels), cotton reels and cheese boxes (heads or wheels), yoghurt pots (hats), pipe cleaners, string or drinking straws (arms and legs), plastic bottles (heads or bodies), and strips cut from washing-up-liquid bottles (arms or tentacles).

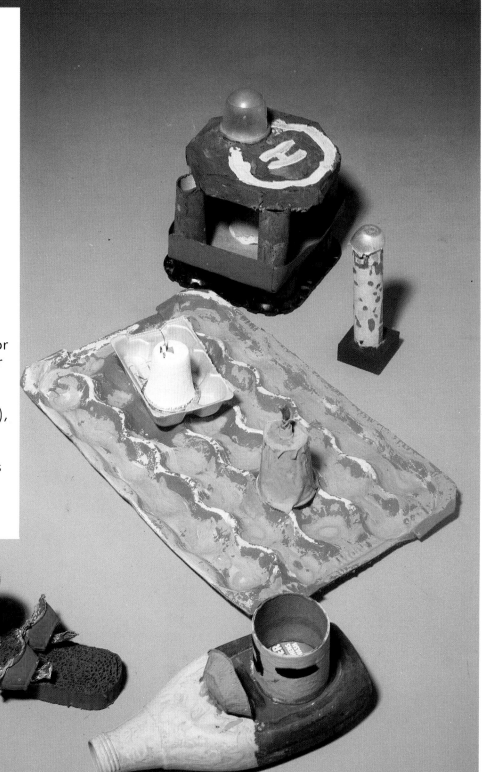

Toys and sculptures

Newspaper Trees
Roll up a sheet of newspaper and sellotape it lightly at one end to hold the roll in place. At the other end, use a pair of scissors to cut the roll into strips (from the centre out). Cut the strips about two-thirds down the length of the roll. Pull up the inside 'leaves', turning them slightly as you pull. The outside 'leaves' will spread out into the shape of a tree.

Whizzer Wheel
Cut out a circle of card (with a diameter of about 12 cm or 5 inches) and paint coloured shapes on it. Bore two holes in the centre and thread a piece of wool through them. Tie the wool so that the wheel is in the middle of two loops. Put each hand through a loop, and twist the wool as much as you can, holding one hand still while turning the other. Pull sharply so that the card spins round, then let it slacken. Continue jerking the wool and the wheel will spin.

Spinning Top
Cut out a circle of card and paint a pattern on it. An older child might try painting a spiral—you could draw the edges in first in pencil. Put a cocktail stick or pencil through the *centre* of the card and spin it.

Windmill
Paint or print bright patterns on both sides of a piece of thin card, about 15 cm or 6 inches square. Cut the paper from each corner to within about 2.5 cm or 1 inch of the centre, as shown.

Without creasing the paper, pull the left side of each corner into the centre. Thread a piece of fuse wire through all the layers of card at the centre, and twist the wire around a bead to secure the front.

Finally, thread a second bead onto the back and attach the wire firmly to the end of a stick.

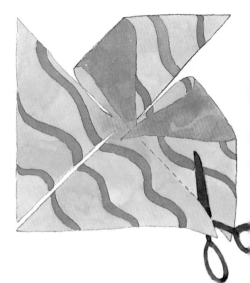

Creeping Cotton Reels

Paint an empty cotton reel and put a thick rubber band through the hole. Place a short pencil inside each end of the band. Wind up one side, put the cotton reel on the table and watch it creep along.

Hole Sculptures

You will need some clay or plasticine to make a base, some tubes, and pieces of paper and card with holes cut in them.

Make some holes in the clay base with a pencil—make some of the holes go straight through the base. Push the cards, tubes and paper into the clay around the holes.

As an alternative, build up a sculpture using straws, toffee papers, chocolate-box wrappings and other see-through materials.

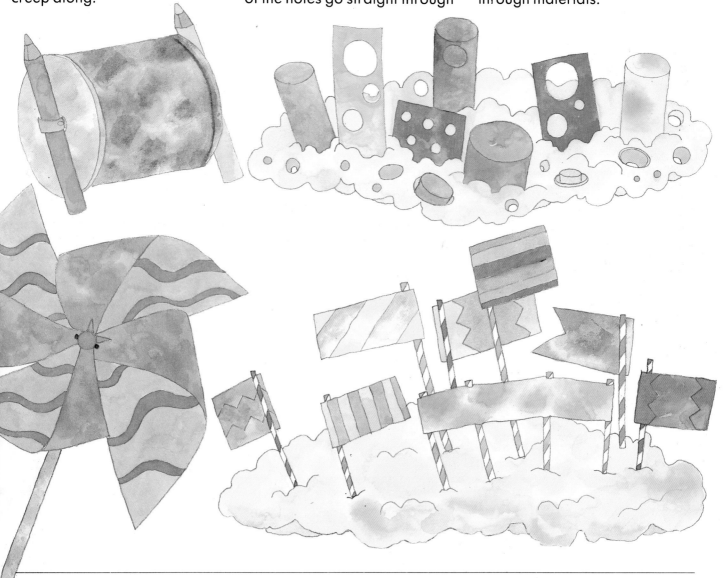

Mobiles

As well as making these for fun, they are also a pleasure to look at. An older child can be encouraged to make one for any babies in the family.

   Cut out some shapes from card or coloured paper. (You can buy coloured foil wrapping paper and stick this onto the card so that it catches the sunlight, or decorate the card with bright colours or a collage.)

   Thread the shapes with cotton and hang them from threaded triangles of drinking straws, or two coat hangers tied together. To balance properly, the shapes need to be tied to both ends and/or to the centre of the hangers.

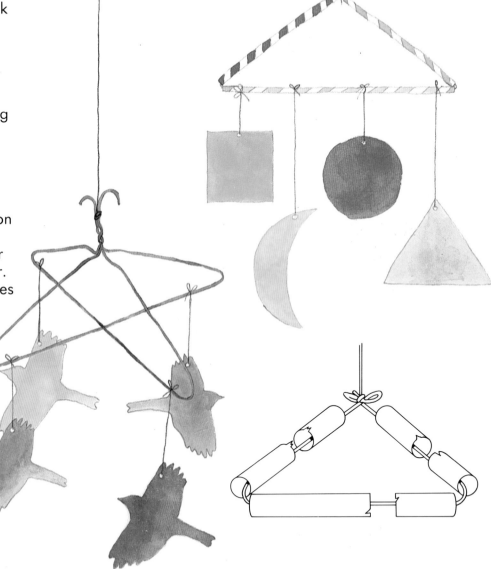

Papier-mâché

Half-fill a washing-up bowl with wallpaper paste and cut up some small strips of newspaper. Smear the object that you want to make a model from with vaseline. Dip the strips of newspaper, one at a time, into the paste and lay the strips over the model base until it is covered with several layers of paper. Leave to dry.

A Paper Plate
Grease the top of an old china plate with vaseline. Cover the top of the plate with papier-mâché strips. When dry, trim the edges with a pair of scissors and remove the china plate from underneath.

A Mask
Grease half an inflated balloon and cover that half with papier-mâché. Allow to dry, then burst the balloon and remove it.

Trim the edges of the mask. Cut out the eye holes and paint on the decorations. You could also glue on some wool or fur bits for hair. Make two small holes on either side of the mask and thread through some elastic to tie the mask in place.

Paper Animals
Completely grease an inflated balloon and cover it with papier-mâché. When dry, glue on cardboard legs, ears and tail, and paint.

A play house

Use a large cardboard box
from an electrical shop (such as
a refrigerator or washing-
machine box). You can either
leave the box whole, and simply
cut a door in one side and a
window in another. Or, cut off
the top and bottom and open
out the four sides. Cut two
windows in the sides and stand
it upright in the corner of a
room. Prop one end against the
wall, or tape it to the wall if
possible, but leave the other end
open to act as a doorway. You
could drape an old sheet over
the top as a roof, and use
smaller boxes for furniture.

An obstacle course

You can make this for dolls or, if you have the space, for children.

For dolls, use cardboard boxes, matchboxes and scraps of material. For children use chairs, stools, cushions, cardboard boxes, old sheets or rugs and pieces of newspaper.

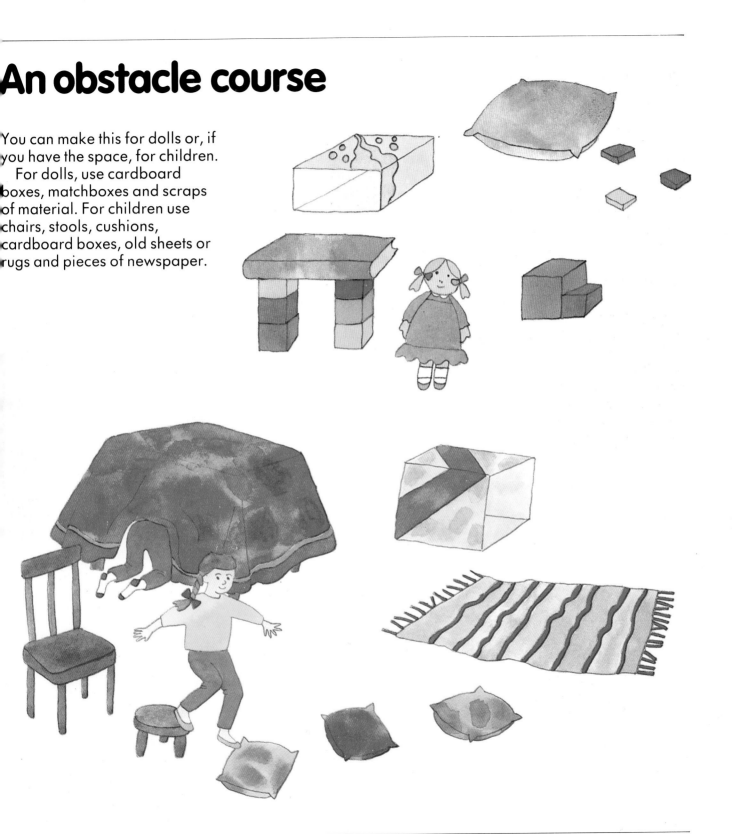

A doll's house

Cut off the tops of four cardboard boxes and glue them together to make the four rooms of a 'house'. (Cardboard wine boxes tend to be a standard size, so try your local off-licence.) Add a touch of realism by cutting out windows and doorways to connect one room with another.

Decorate the boxes with scraps of wallpaper or pieces from a discarded wallpaper-sample book. Furnish the rooms with objects from your art box. Some ideas are shown in the illustrations below and on the opposite page.

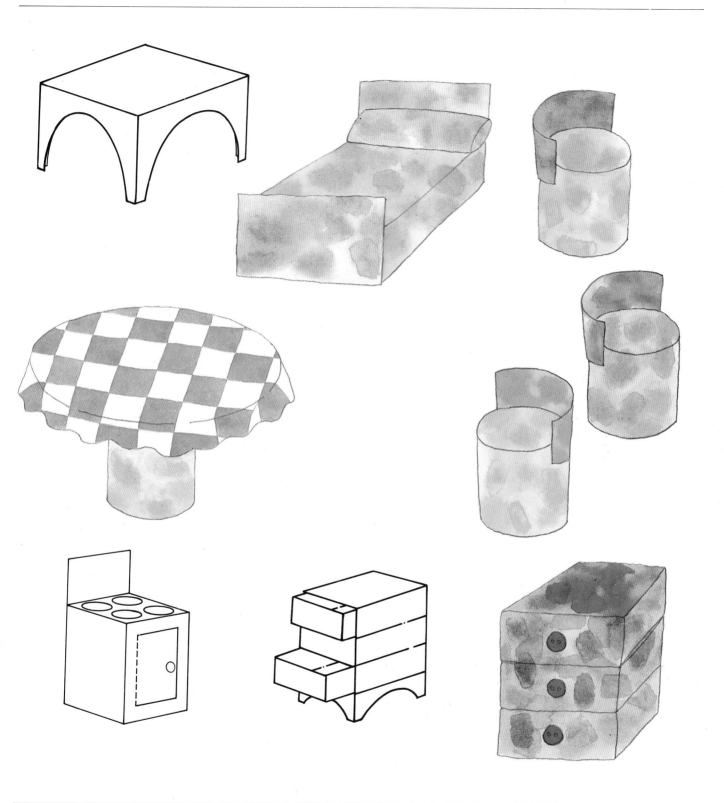

Threading and tying

Shoe Lacing

Draw a large boot onto a piece of card, or trace over the outline of the drawing shown here. Punch holes in the top of the boot and practise threading and tying shoe laces, as with an ordinary shoe.

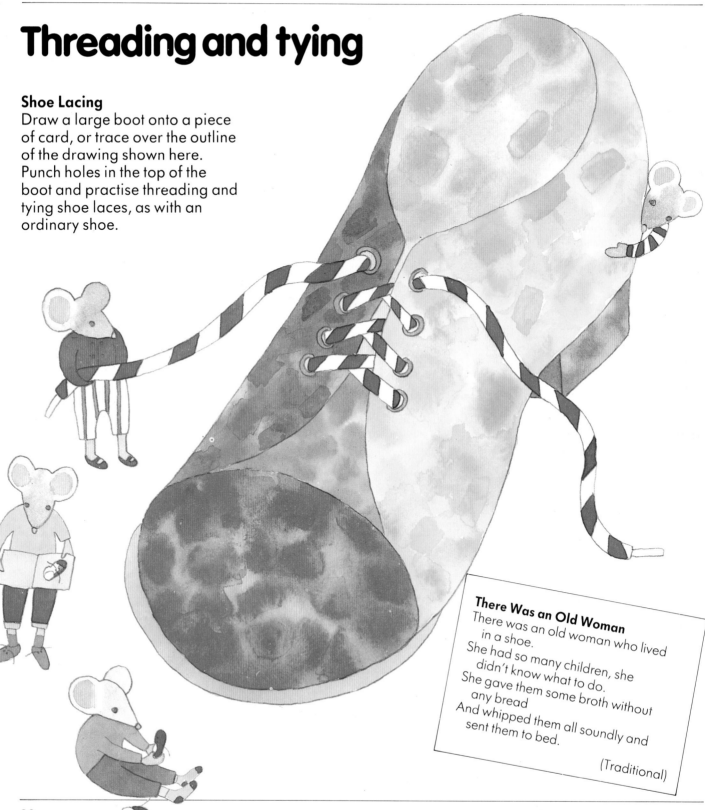

There Was an Old Woman

There was an old woman who lived in a shoe.
She had so many children, she didn't know what to do.
She gave them some broth without any bread
And whipped them all soundly and sent them to bed.

(Traditional)

Threading

1 Cut out a simple shape from a firm piece of cardboard, then cut or punch holes large enough for shoelaces to be threaded through to make a pattern.

2 Trace the shape of your child's name onto a card with punched holes. Thread through the holes with coloured shoelaces.

3 Glue a picture with a clear outline onto a piece of card. Punch large holes all around the edge of the picture (about ½ cm or ¼ inch apart). Help your child to stitch round the picture with a bodkin (a large blunt needle) and wool.

4 Take some cotton reels, or yoghurt pots with holes cut in the bottom, and thread them onto string to make a snake. (Make knots in the string to keep the yoghurt pots apart.)

Older children can thread macaroni (or other types of hollow pasta), pieces of coloured straws, foil bottle tops and beads onto long shoelaces.

Woollen Balls

Cut out two circles of card the same size, and make a medium-sized hole in the middle of each. Put the two card rings together and wind a ball of wool through the middle and around the rings.

When the layers of wool nearly fill the centre hole, cut them by sliding the scissors between the two pieces of card. When you have cut the wool all the way round, pull the pieces of card a little way apart and tie a strong piece of wool firmly round the middle. Then remove the cards.

A Woolly Chicken

Make a woollen ball as above. Fold a pipe cleaner in half and hook it through the wool, before you tie it in the middle and remove the card rings. Use a long piece of wool to tie the middle and leave the two ends dangling for the moment.

Make a smaller ball, and tie the middle of this ball with the same piece of wool that you used to tie the larger one. Shape the pipe cleaners into legs, and stick a felt or cardboard beak onto the head.